YO-DKM-130

Distilled Lives

VOLUME FOUR

2018

Illinois State Poetry Society

Kathleen Robinson, Editor

Associate Editors

Susan T. Moss   Judith Tullis   Susan Auld   Frank Hubeny

Cover design by Kathy Lohrum Cotton

Cover photograph, "Newly Hatched Monarch," by G. Prentice

Interior design by Kathleen Robinson

Printed in the United States of America
by Kindle Direct Publishing

Published October 2018

ISBN-13: 978-1726694247

Poetry is life distilled.

— Gwendolyn Brooks

Illinois Poet Laureate, 1968-2000

CONTENTS

FOREWORD

On November 3, 2018, we launched *Distilled Lives Volume Four* and celebrated the twenty-seventh anniversary of ISPS as a nationally chartered poetry society at our third Gala held in the Park Ridge Country Club. Seventy-three members' poems fill this newest edition with diverse genres including haibun and haiku, all ongoing variations of interpreting our lives. Readings by participating poets debuted the collection.

Illinois State Poetry Society dates back to the early 1970s, and its legacy has grown from one chapter to the present seven that meet in public libraries statewide. We also have an increased number of out-of-state poets and leadership in the National Federation of State Poetry Societies.

Currently, the ISPS board includes Susan T. Moss, President and chapter facilitator: Northbrook; Jim Lambert, Vice-President; Melissa Huff, Secretary; Judith Tullis, Treasurer; and Frank Hubeny, Historian. Chapter Facilitators are Susan T. Moss, Northbrook, Susan Auld, haiku chapter, Northbrook; Barbara Eaton, Lisle; Kathy Cotton, Carbondale; Caroline Johnson, Darien; Kathleen Robinson, Champaign; Kathleen Murphy, Pontiac; and Sheila Kirscher, at-large member.

Included in the effort to reach out to members, ISPS offers a website maintained and managed by Alan Harris. This site gives poets the opportunity to post their poems and stay informed of chapter meetings and special events.

As a state society, we strive to promote, share and support the writing and reading of poetry. Our nonprofit organization recognizes the multiple voices and individual talents of all its members. *Distilled Lives Volume Four* is the latest effort to lift the human spirit and share creative endeavors to make this world a better place.

Susan T. Moss, President
Illinois State Poetry Society
Fall 2018

the right path
  zigzagging
into a clearing

olive trees bristle
in the shadow
of bulldozers

rubble
  a child picks up a toy
collateral damage

flags of victory
hover over
my son's hollow grave

on the face of a child...bomb strikes

enemy
fire
friendly
fire
same
sorrow

Play with Me

I don't care what you're doing
don't care what you say
somehow, someway
I'll get you to play
with me

Put down the remote
turn off that TV
leave the recliner
play with me

I'll get my ball
sit next to the door
then bark, as I let it
roll 'cross the floor

Come on now
that's your cue
I grow tired
waiting for you
I'm a dog
what else can I do

Sometimes I wish
I could talk
Perhaps at least then
we'd go for a walk

Save What We Can

It's snowing
the wind's blowing
and I drive home knowing
I have no place to go

Thoughts
keep racing
through my mind

Wife lost her job
we fell behind
Another one
she couldn't find
How could I
have been so blind

I knew this day would come
but the mortgage folks said
they would give us
more time

I turn the corner
and from my seat
see all our belongings
there on the street

I love that woman
she's so sweet
Even now through tears
with a hug she greets

The kids are at school
we are in luck
Save what we can
on the back of the truck

At Peace

See me now
or forever close your eyes
blinded to my soul

Hear me this moment
as my song of peace resonates
with your dreams of love

Touch my mind with
your essence of strength and hope
and open my heart to
satiating, eternal, selfless love

Tomorrow is here,
just come near
and hold my hand
as we listen to silence,
while I wrap my arms
around your heart
and kiss your eyes
in quiet, meek gentleness

Maria's Broken Heart

Your arm hangs lifeless
by the side of your bed,
your breasts bare, childless.
Your long, black hair touches the floor.

Maria's died of a broken heart,
for her there will be pain no more.

Tears have washed your perfect face,
a mother-to-be with no baby to embrace.
Cruel reality that most women fear,
no first cry, but silence behind the closed door.

Maria's died of a broken heart,
for her there will be pain no more.

I saw you sleeping as I entered the room,
wondered why everyone was weeping,
not knowing what took place before.
Then my mother explained,
"Maria's died of a broken heart,
for her there will be pain no more."

As children, we're not able to comprehend,
but I tried to find answers and understand
how one's heart can break
over losing the life they adore.

Maria's died of a broken heart.
For her there will be no more.

Dysphoria 1

Why in silence do I still sit distraught?
Wishing my secret find freedom and flight,
yearning to give my heart long-clouded sight?
Husband, father, soldier—in wars I fought.
Jailed in wrong body, soul forever fraught.
Lawn mower, your steed, slices morning light.
Your lithe body calls my love to alight
on your shoulder like a mourning dove caught
without hope to change wrong body for life.
With you my knight, worlds join in dew freshness.
Dove's mournful call transformed to triumphant fife.
Your wave to my balcony lifts sadness.
It flies heart to hope, to love, without strife.

Lucky

I remember her clumping tread,
the rubber-tipped cane
striking the floor before
the halt slide step.

In a hurry, it was a faster
clump-shush, clump-shush.
As a child, I never understood
why she walked that way.

She'd had polio, her childhood
spent in heavy leg braces,
one leg forever shorter,
lucky she could walk at all.

Her feet were tiny, her shoes
built-up, special ordered,
bought to match her wardrobe
and walking stick.

Her gait sounded an early
warning system to teenage ears.
Later it was white noise
of her invisibility.

Now, with belated empathy
I swipe cobwebs from her cane,
long consigned to an attic corner—
put to use for my shattered knee,

lucky I can walk at all.

Dementia

Baptized by her own fire, water too tepid for redemption,
she had lived in every house on that crowded lane,
remembered each one as if she could return at any time.

Old acquaintances floated in and out of the rooms
like ghosts she could speak to now with dignity,
re-writing conversations, changing outcomes.

Bluebirds nested in her hair, but she combed out the twigs,
stored them on shelves, tasted the venom of serpents
she wrestled, then ran from, 'til mud filled her shoes.

As she rewrote all the stories, a phantom overtook
her, burnt down the houses on that crowded lane,
and she couldn't find her way there again.

crocus bloom
finding the right word
in a new language

still summer air
the wind song
of a hummingbird's wings

black birds
on winter cattails
ink stone dusk

unpacking—
the mountains stay
folded inside me

empty of clouds i float to the stars

shaping
the empty sky
starlings

Seven Minutes

In seven minutes you can
talk with a friend, listen to music,
eat pancakes, do the dishes—

a mere seven minutes.
passing so quickly, inconsequential,
until a stranger explains to you

how they did all they could do
but because your beautiful daughter
was under the water for seven minutes . . . .

You couldn't have known,
he says. There's nothing
you could have done, he says.

That inconsequential number
is all it takes to lose someone you love
in the room right next to you, on a day

that should have been ordinary—
leaving you to a life forever changed
into increments of seven minutes.

Forever Autumn
For Gage, 11/8/2005 – 10/31/2007

Autumn, always my favorite,
begins and ends too quickly.
It briefly ushers in the year's end—
colorful leaves a pictorial
of everything God can do.
The air, a sensory experience,
both tranquil and crisp
like the scent of fresh linen.
Scampering animals foraging
for those days on the horizon.

I've come here to share
this autumn day with you,
to say Happy Birthday
and watch the leaves turn to gold.
It's truly a beautiful sight, a
day any grandmother would
want to share with her grandson.
I'm sure you would love it, even though
this year would mark your first as
a teenager. No longer a little boy, a
handsome young man. At least that's
what I see. In reality you will be forever
turning two. Like the colors of autumn,
your season brief. Forever beautiful.
Forever Autumn.

Wedding

It was a hot day in mid summer when our seven-year-old daughter
decided to get married. She wore her communion dress and veil, the
long white stockings. The groom, also seven, wore his only suit.
The priest, our oldest son, wore his altar boy red and white.
The bridesmaid, her sister, made a dandelion chain for her hair
and carried sweet peas. The youngest brother held the flag.

When her father and I looked out the window and saw them gathered
in the rose garden, we stood gape-mouthed—bride and groom
kneeling in the dirt, the priest blessing them. It was then I saw the
flower girls, their bouquets of roses, daisies, bachelor buttons,
zinnias, baby's breath and some boxwood, our vases bereft. My
husband snapped a photo just before the bride came running toward
the house, sobbing. *I don't want to marry him. Make it stop.*

a dab of perfume—
fragrance
of summers past

At Saylesville Pond
Just as we take the train to get to Tarascon or Rouen,
we take death to reach a star. —Vincent Van Gogh

The poignancy of this spring morning falls heavy as I replay the
doctor's words: *This is the last trip she will take.* I sit on the iron
bench by the pond—frozen with the thought of her dying,
living with her absence.

water over stone
the splash of a carp
caught in the sun

Along the reedy fringes of the marsh, dragonflies hover over
dankness to mate. One darts forward, then back, spirals down only
to be towed upward by a male, a path difficult to follow. My eyes
rest on the aluminum boat anchored to the dock, quiet seeping into
me like medicine. A glint of orange flits around the milkweed.
A breeze brushes my shoulder, startles me with its breath and
I wonder if it really does take death to reach a star.

oars stilled…
a raven's hoarse "scree"
scratches the air

Autumn-Kissed

Smack
in the middle
of the window pane
still wet with autumn's rain,
one golden yellow leaf,
the last of the front yard birch—
clinging
waiting
   on the outside
      of the morning.

In Her Own Time

Tall and spindly, she stands behind
her sunny neighbors of summer,
a backdrop for their zinnious beauty,
waiting for her time to come.

Amid their late August goodbyes,
she quietly shows her face
as gently she nods
while pansies bow out.

Right on time, she greets September
in purple straw hat,
swaying with lifting breezes,
savoring short crisp days,
knowing autumn waits in the wings.

Like a petite purple star, grounded
in a chorus of plenty, she watches
green turn to crimson and bronze, listens
to the crunching steps of passersby, feels
October winds twirl around and about her.

Through sun, rain, unpredictable days
and frosty November nights,
she lingers for "the last dance."

Her name? Just *Aster*.

My Caldero

On the precious big burner
of my stove, you sit with pride
wearing stains from burnt drips
of fiery fish stew or curried okra,
nudging away the blue tea kettle.

Your cast aluminum carapace
can take some serious heat,
making me fall in love with you
whenever I cook, yet I hide your
ugliness when company comes.

With you dangling at my hip,
I could have visited Frieda's
Mexican Blue Cottage to cook
goat stew for her below her window,
to soothe her broken body and soul.

We could have visited Gabriel
Marquez to cook for his lunch some
yellow rice, fragrant with *soffritto*.
The crusty rice at the bottom
of your belly could be a potion
for spinning magical daydreams.

We could have gone to Cavafy to cook
for him rice pilaf as he longed for
the return journey to Ithaca. Like him
there is no home for me in my birthplace.
I console my soul by cooking sweet
Pulao rice in your dependable belly.

A Witching Hour

The ancient tapestry of inky sky
hung before the window. Stillness
thickened as the tireless sea thrashed
down below on the steep black rock.

It sang the same hymn to memory,
eulogizing beaches I walked barefoot.

Once on a raw sienna beach I roamed
with my children, chasing terns
while flapping our beach towels. Nearby,
ice cream cake cottages dozed.

Squeezing my toes against the sand
on Ipanema beach, I watched lean men,
and women with fat bottoms. On hilltop,
Christ the Redeemer raised his arms to fly.

The memory of the powdery white sand
of Gulf Island dazzled in darkness.
Ancient Fort Pickens loomed large.
Setting sorrows aside, I wept in delight.

The First Wedding

We wed at ten o'clock.
Your mother's voice soft—
for the first time,
my father and his wife
nearby and unpleasant.

"Do you take . . . ."
said the Justice of the Peace,
the same voice that performed
my mother's funeral.

The ceremony so quick,
but I thought our marriage
would last forever.

That's not the way it was
at all.

If I Were a Cavewoman

If I were a cavewoman
I wouldn't have a fire,
wouldn't own or make
a pot to cook in.
I'd live on berries and dirt
if I were a cavewoman.

If I lived during that time
when there were no showers,
I wouldn't bathe in the ocean
or river or communal pool
nor use animal fat and blood.
I'd sponge down with water only
and use the perfume of flowers.

If I were a cavewoman
I'd find an empty cave,
hide from the men that wouldn't
put up with my behavior, because
if I were a cavewoman—
I wouldn't last long.

Puffs of Smoke

Who are we but
puffs of smoke
from the gentle pipe of an old man
sitting at the Cape of Good Hope
at the southern tip of the African continent
watching the nearby penguins nest and play
in his ever-expanding mind,
a dreamer thinking of things
and places far away,
mulling the idea of unfurling
life upon the land
and watching it grow by leaps
and bounds,
rolling good and evil down the slope
together to see how the raucous wrestling
match turns out,
smiling at what will be and where the
journey might lead,
he longs for company,
for laughter and joy in the long dark night,
and welcomes the sun he's just made with
open arms and a full heart of sparkling diamonds each day.

Without Electricity

Without electricity
where would we be,
moving about the streets
like dizzy unshackled prisoners,
bumping into each other
with wide eyes and outstretched hands,
free of devices and looking out
at colors, trees, birds, and
beautiful white clouds dotting
the sky like songs waiting to be heard.
We might go for a walk
or read a book
or sit on a swing and feel
the wind blowing leaves past our feet
and soft sunshine within our minds,
a powerless yet empowering place to be,
dancing alone with others
away from the lights
and into the moonglow,
looking for crumbs that feed the soul
and tapping joyful toes to the beat of
an unplugged-in existence,
the inner electric switch turned on
and dialed into the universe,
crackling with the big boundless
beauty of love.

For My Unborn Grandchild

I am a song of longing

to inhale your new-baby scent,
to stroke the soft spot on your scalp,
soothe your wails until your eyes
have shut like tiny windows.

I long to hold you on my lap
and read you illustrated tales,
though paper books may be extinct
as mastadons by then.

I long to help you with your homework.
though you may not be able
to spell or do math
without an app.

I long to take you to see an opera,
to hear an orchestra perform,
though you may find the music foreign
as a dial phone or a VCR.

I am a song of longing
with an accompaniment of terror

that sometime you will go to school,
to a movie or a shopping mall,
and not return, another statistic
on the six-o'clock news.

Sudden Death

After the shock has dimmed a bit
like the twilit sky,
everything gains weight.

Your toothbrush turns to lead, your bar
of shower soap transforms to stone.
Your coffee mug is suddenly
a carillon bell turned upside down.

At work, the well-intentioned words
of colleagues hit the ground
like hail. Your concentration,
grown fat from a diet of wretchedness,
requires a cane to put one foot

in front of the other. A rhino
sits on your memory, and your energy,
once as fleet as a cheetah,
tumbles into a vat of cement.

Only your sleep loses pound after pound
until its clothes grow much too large
and flap in the random gusts of your grief.

solstice evening
cicadas chant twilight
into stars

red darkroom light
her profile
among the negatives

crow caws
in the evening mist
the solstice moon

damned quick
the odd grey hair
finding friends

in mass the pomp and circumstance of black holes

jack o'lantern
the man-in-the-moon's
zombie smile

What Would I Write Tomorrow?

You ask,
What do you write about?
Where does your
inspiration come from?
What would you write tomorrow?
Well, my friend, this moment
of tomorrow's song
is today blessings all along.
Look above, below,
and within to see—
awareness is the golden key.
Each moment of silence
brings stillness in thoughts
of peaceful nonviolence.
Let it be, your daily guidance.
For what is not heard,
nor seen, nor felt
is an inner knowing—
present stillness
bringing oneness of thoughts,
beauty in words, forever sought.
Think of tomorrow . . . . Why?
This is today.
Know inner presence is near,
listen to whispering words so clear
coming from within you, dear.
Be still and hear. Yes, you are the seer.
Tomorrow's time is now,
each second past, a memory
of what was written last.
I write of tomorrow, for it is today.
Live in the "moment of now,"
don't let it slip away.

Slow-Rising Illinois Spring

At this southern edge,
where her bare feet
dangle in the roiled merge

of two mighty rivers,
spring shimmies up early
from Kentucky, suns to life

inaugural crocus and Bradford pear,
daffodil and forsythia yellows,
blush of redbud, dogwood, cherry.

Up the spine of I-57,
scent of lilac rolls 400 miles north
through her seed-corn hungry belly

toward big-city shoulders, dusted
with the last of road salt and snow:
slow rising, Illinois spring.

Breaking the Fast

I have loved
night's last black hour
as the universe

lifts invisible hands
to break the egg of morning
into Earth's iron skillet—

orange yolk on the horizon,
whites spreading thin,
sizzling into the sky.

My appetite is sparked
for the feast
of another day,

the end
of a long night's
empty plate.

Winter Dim

Gusts and ice pellets,
then slant of snow
blur the window,
attack the hollow oak that once
cradled my childhood swing.

I wander for a few moments,
smell fresh-mown grass,
finger plum blossoms beneath
unblemished sky, and follow
bluebird song.

Yesterday, a straw hat for
covering my gray hair hung
in the mud room. Today, as I rub
my arms, dry from itchy wool,
early dusk settles on the keyboard.

Unworn white lawn mitigates
black sky. Winds through the cedar
cease their swoosh, snowfall lightens.

The tea kettle blows fog.
As I rise, my knees jerk from
advancing age. I pass through
a spider thread, avoiding my old hound
who snores into tomorrow.

Sitting down for tea, I sip ennui
and reach for a novel, popular during
my prime, in large print now.

My Routine

I wake to loose threads
dangling in my head.
From the bay window,

barely visible limbs of
a solitary poplar fan the air.
A train rumbles through the blur.

In my prairie town,
coffee percolates
black and gray moments.

I walk out into the chill
stumbling through twigs
and crusty leaves.

Through the maze of day,
I touch shoulders with tall shadows,
hear invisible robins.

With the maple leaves,
street lights change from
green to yellow to red.

Home at night,
I destroy pesky cobwebs
with my feather duster,

settle into my armchair.
Beating time in waning lamplight
to folk songs playing

in my childhood,
I drift into another dawn.

Fairy Tale First Responder

The call came from Dispatch:
wild animal attack. Two
hikers reported hearing
screams and sounds of
violence from an address
at the edge of the woods—
which is never good,
but this was the worst
I'd ever seen and I've seen lots.
I arrived in the ambulance
ready to assist any injured
and wounded as the police
broke down the door.
Gore everywhere. Some crazy
hunter gone mad with an axe.
He sat slumped over, breathing
hard, while blood dripped from
long gashes on his arms and legs.
Hunks of fur were littered about
and piles of flesh with large splinters
of wood from furniture that got in the
way of the axe. The first victim,
an unconscious elderly female
covered in slime and blood.
The second was a female child
similarly coated. Conscious
but in shock, she sat rocking
herself and holding her arms
tightly across her chest. Her red
hoodie sweatshirt pulled over her head,
eyes staring vacantly,
she murmured,
Wolf.

Sandy Hook, Orlando, Las Vegas
A Golden Shovel using a line from T.S. Eliot's
"The Love Song of J. Alfred Prufrock"

News screams another mass shooting and I **do**
not know what to do. How can **I**
stop the gun violence or **dare**
oppose the NRA and rabid Right **to**
ban automatic weapons? Bullets **eat**
victims in a bloody banquet, not giving **a**
damn if you are black, brown, yellow or **peach**.

From A Midsummer Night's Dream: A "Snake Poem"
The poet's pen . . . gives to airy nothing a local habitation
and a name.   V, 1, 15–16

The first thing a magician learns is that
there is no magic. The **poet's** lesson,
a similar one, concerns her perfumed **pen**.
It is not ink, paper, nor pen which **gives**
the poet her special magic. "**To** sleep,
perchance to dream . . . ." We're **airy** spirits all.
The will o' th' wisp is something/**nothing**;
the paradox **a** poet's provenance.
The **local** bricklayer's advice: to write
a living line, sweat blood. **Habitation**
and home hath she non, save Mount Helicon.
The critic roars, "Would she had blotted **a**
thousand!" Woman, scribbler, a poet's **name**.

Psalm

I was afraid I had forgotten you,
my love, it has been so long.
Will I recognize your face?
I have suffered in my loneliness
more than I can say.
The truth is, I have forgotten myself,
I have forgotten my own life.
Please, my dearest love,
help me to remember.
Let us meet face to face. . .
In remembering you
I will remember my own soul.

My Uncle

My Uncle Bruce is a special guy.
I love my Uncle, I do!
And the very best part, straight from the heart,
he really loves me, too.

Although his beard can be really scratchy
on my soft and tender skin,
it's worth it just to have him near
and see his big wide grin.

He's known as Mr. Fixit Man,
so give him any chore
and he will prove without a doubt
there's nothing he can't restore.

He always has a sense of humor,
and's so fun to be around,
but he's also very smart indeed
and utters things profound.

Yes, I love my Uncle Bruce,
and even though he's hairy,
I think you will agree with me,
he's extraordinary!

If I Could Become a Building

Buildings are marvelous structures
whether modern or antique.
Each and every one, like me,
is special and unique.

If I became a building, I wonder
which kind would I be?
What earthly purpose would I serve?
Would others find shelter in me?

Would I provide a sturdy foundation
so others would be secure,
safe from harmful destruction,
and the storms of life to endure?

Would my windows always be bright and clear,
with an unobstructed view,
to give me an inspirational vision
of what I am called to do?

Would the inside décor bring peace and comfort
to all who visit there?
Would the ambiance radiate beauty and love
to let them know that I care?

If I were a building, I'd love to be
a church, a haven of rest,
a welcoming place of love and forgiveness
where everyone is blessed.

From the Poetess to the Reader
translated by Mary Ann Eiler from her French poem
"De la poètesse au lecteur"

I am the union of secrets,
a charmer of words.

I transform ash to snow.

When night comes,
I slumber in your eyes.

I give you a lover's suite in strophes.

You experience me in mind,
not in flesh.

I forgive the unsaid.

The black heart of absence
beats between my lines.

Thrilled in your hands,
I remain ever discreet.

I address the shadows of your chagrin.

Wed me, then, make love
to me between my sheets.

With my demise, I rest at ease,
luring another to give me a read.

The Vagaries of Love
To the poetess Marceline Desbords-Valmore
1786–1859

translated by Mary Ann Eiler from
her French poem "Les caprices de l'amour"

a mistress beyond shame
a petulant lover
make night-fire
scorching the heart's skin

the thick snow of sleep
dawn's avalanche
loud word-flows of slush (his)
mute metaphors of frost (hers)

in turn, all destroyed
at the drowning of the sun
in the swell of a cold kiss

a casket full of roses

a formidable charmer
the nape of your neck
interacting with my fingers
eyes reaching deep within
we kissed away full moons
which seemed within our adolescent grasp

I lassoed your scent
with my imagination
and then fell into a chasm of foolish engagement
all the while betrothed to the idea

that the old car's heater
would warm us into eternity
even after our lips grew cold

bottle of next time

exposed affections
cheeks explode crimson embarrassment
eyes defect
hide in dark brown retina
beleaguered heart kisses another potential
goodbye
before the hello is registered

shy flowers close buds under intrusive sun
reopening unavailable
until next spring
and still that is an uneven
conclusion

when balance renders itself
as steady as a wino's dance

Discourse

Maybe we lost our tails
Maybe we lost a rib
It doesn't matter how
we got here, what matters
is how we treat each other
Maybe kindness is
the highest praise

The Nine

I chanced upon them
on a sunny day
unchallenged by clouds.
I was looking for
some peace, some
sign of goodness
in the universe.

They were out early,
their white heads
dotting the blue sky
like an undiscovered
constellation in the bare trees.

Black robes over
broad avian shoulders
revealed only when
one of them moved.

What brought nine
eagles to hold court
on this river bank?
I had hoped to see one,
maybe two.

I couldn't imagine
anything so supreme
as these nine eagles
watching ice flows
on the river as
spring slowly
approached.

Buffalo Crossing

I sit atop this butte,
binoculars deployed,
as the buffalo
cross the cold blue
stream, the queue belly-high,
spittle dripping from wet
mouths, calves wading
close to their cows,
headed where they
need to go, through
orange sage, half-green hills.

Their lonely trek
made as winter wanes—
what tells them it's time
to cross into spring's lush green?

Would that my own
life-crossings resembled these.

Autumn on Whitefish River

My favorite place along the river
is a bend where the rapids do not rush.

Yet the flow is strong and steady
and seems to speak to me of life.

Cedars turn a deeper, richer red,
junipers and spruces sprinkle down

their cones and needles. Shards
of bark and twists of leaves resist

the stream's persistent pull and push,
then relent, give in and float on down,

adding to a pile of brush and logs
the beavers made. As I rest upon

the river's fragrant edge, my arms
and chin atop my knees, I soak into

my blood something barely audible.
I strain to hear a truth whispered low—

within the play of water, wind and time,
my life floats by like needles off the pine.

Progression

My wife said I'd gone
haiku cuckoo, I just said
I'd gone haikuku

Haiku: a three-line
Ah so! Japanese poem
heightening little

Lowku: a western
imitation—forced to fit,
an eyeful lot missed

Maiku: my own blend
of oriental stricture,
occidental *mot*

My wife says now I'm
maiku cuckoo, I say I've
become maikuku

Poets
with apologies to Joyce Kilmer

I see that I shall never know
a tree as lovely as a poet.

A poet's hungry mouth is blessed
with words, not food, at his behest.

A poet may in summer bear
a robin's droppings in her hair.

A poet hears God's muse all day
condemned to work at what to say.

But trees are made to fit the rule,
and God lets poets play the fool.

Listen to That Mother Sing Her Baby to Sleep

What do you suppose that young mother
expects him to do with a mockingbird—
nuisance of an imitative thing?
Whether it can sing or not, bound to make a mess
flying around the nursery pecking at the child's fingers.

As alternative, a diamond ring is no age-appropriate toy.
Flashy, ostentatious, even in brass it's a choking hazard.
But it gets worse. Why give a looking glass to a baby,
encourage vanity or risk the poor thing's
having to crawl over shards of broken glass?

Now, a billy goat is a nice pet for an older child,
but for a newborn? And why a billy,
not even a source of back-up goat's milk?
What is she thinking with this cart and bull?
She's considered the probability of a high-speed

turnover, baby flung to the sky. If her child
survives the ride behind an irascible bull,
I suppose a puppy would be a consolation,
but not one of those annoying little yappy dogs.
It's as if making a ruckus were all Rover's good for.

If he doesn't bark he's to be cast aside like
the billy goat that balked at giving cart rides.
This mother's obsessed with animal wagons!
Finally she promises a horse and cart,
but anticipates it breaking down like all the others.

Perhaps he'll get to keep the pony till he gets older.
At last, the only thing this baby receives
are his mother's hyperbolic endearments—
all she needed to offer in the first place
since he's not quieted by diamonds or wagon rides.

Death by Poetry

When they opened her up
she was riddled with alliterative lines.
They didn't even try to transcribe.
They just sewed her up again and sent her home.
Three months later, in the spring of the year,
she died of poems, her body alive with them,
protest poems in her spleen,
holy psalms of praise in folds
of her brain's gray matter,
love lyrics' pulsing residual rhythm
through both auricles of her enlarged heart,
arteries clogged with blockage,
her lungs so cloudy with misted images
each breath must have been a labor,
her breasts, hard as on the third day
    when the milk comes in,
    engorged with poems she could not let down,
benign syllables in situ—tight cyclic haiku,
ruptured confessional poems
spilling infectious mixed metaphor
    into her abdominal cavity,
an ectopic sonnet that could not gestate,
    poised to burst the tube that stretched in
    holding in its will to life,
parasitic poems, plagiarized and feeding
    on the good bacteria,
one last magnificent poem, almost spoken,
lodged in her throat like a piece of steak.
Say only that she died of beauty undigested
    like rough rubies.
We need only read her death to be gifted of it all.

Spirit Islands

Will they release their magic
these mountains where rain pours
silver manna from the unknown

Will they release their magic
these oceans opening infinite
golden homes of diamonds

These waterfalls and pools
untouched except for elves
while even the sun falls
at the feet of the water
and winds stop talking

These forests hosting the clouds
stretch straight and holy trunks
remember each dancing rainbow

Will they release their magic
these islands born out of nowhere
in a ruby cataclysm

Winter Pond

Spring air slides like white orchids
chilled with champagne. I recall
your kiss, soft as swans' breath.
When I look for you, I see
only your reflection in the pond. Your wings
float upward, kissing cool lips of Moon.

I wait, islanded in my obsession
with poems, as far away as if I'd
moved to Paris. In floating snow I catch songs
of authors gone, Baudelaire or Mallarme.
Magic words drift
past my fingers—yours? A ghost's?

Asleep, dreaming, I touch your misted hair.
You say you love me
yet I gaze into eyes like swans'
that give little away.
I hide my own secrets
under chill perfection of Chablis
and poetry of silver ponds.

In Florida

The color behind my eyelids
turns a mustard hue,
the purplish-red fading—
that Illinois shade I set
by closing my eyes tight.
At night in the dark,
why do the highways
frighten me when weaved
so close to the ocean?
The heat makes it tough
to breathe, in the way
crowded rooms
make me an asthmatic
or a sweaty fool.
My wife says we should
buy a beach house. I'm
just trying to remain
within the white lines.
The water pulls us close,
the guard rail no more a safe
haven than the kitchen knife
your finger bleeds from.
The chances we take,
the discomfort we avoid,
the breath not yet
bestowed upon our lungs.

Humerus

That tree I planted in the first grade is old. Its limbs so
long they touched our yard, traveled now by new feet.
I see the heart I carved when we were young, in love before
we understood the concept. Perpetual climbing for you,
going higher and higher, like the farther I went the more
you'd hold my hand when I descended. Remember the
sound? I remember you yelping and I recall the beautiful
silence of the fall. Sure, it snapped and I'm a permanent
issue in the airport, but remember how you held my hand
the whole way? Both of us crying but together, both of us
sure we'd be okay. Yeah, I'm okay and my arm doesn't
hurt anymore. How are you, love?

The Unfolding

"Old fool" that he was,
his son took his ladder—
thinking the keeping
would no longer matter.

Young fool that he was,
he made his dad sadder.
The old duffer bought
a shiny new ladder.

A clear sunny day,
a shiny new ladder:
there's nary a thing
can make a man gladder.

Out Back

Our backyard is the pleasant place
that we consider spirit space.

It's where our wash can whip and fly,
and stands a little chance to dry,

the place a feisty jenny wren
chooses over fen or glen,

and where we see a robin rest,
among the grapevines, on her nest.

Our backyard's where, atop the fence,
a coon tiptoes without pretense.

It's where the finches fuss and preen
in puddled water 'til they're clean,

the place we read and sit to rock,
where neighbors stop a bit to talk,

and where the rusty wagon carries
pots of ivy, verbena fairies.

Our backyard's where our dreams unfold,
where love comes true, where time's on hold.

Flower Dreams

We dream in flowers
or so it seemed last night,
whole mountain streams of them
cascading in a mad crush
of blue and red and yellow blooms,
brushing wild over our wetted nerves
the way clouds brush under the sky
before a crash of rain.

Yesterday as you walked
the evening's path into the dark of night,
you picked these four wild daisies
on stems of varied lengths
and five of Queen Anne's lace,
cutting all these into
the grip of your other hand
along with varied grasses
until, after bundling all these
into a dirt-cracked Mason jar,
you held them high
as our bouquet
over the table top,
wisps of beauty floating.

At night we sleep
 in long flowers of dreams
that vanish quickly at dawn,
bodiless as clouds.

This, you tell me, is why you smile
over the flowers laced
on the table between us
each morning,
again and again.

Into the Flowers

Put your music into the flowers
and let them play it, one note at a time,
drawing the long bow of desire
across the strings of slow-stepping time.
Then let them rest.

After, they might draw the bow again, again, again,
like a dancer's foot in a slow waltz time, or
as a gardener
pressing the filaments of new roots
deep into the loam.

Then stop.
Be still.
Let the flowers
wait for the music
to seep out of them
like Eros himself,
at first a trickling flow, perhaps—
later, a pouring fountain of it
in a quickened vibrato,
an echoing tremolo,
soft on its hinge of unfolding resonances,
nevertheless surging somehow like prayer,
like prayer slipping into such flowers
and coming to rest.

wildflowers seed
an interminable highway
hitchhikers

picture windows
golfer drives
hole-in-one

gate without a fence
alone against apple tree
fluffy clouds debate

This Thing Called Love

This thing called love
    that speaks from the grave
and bids remembrance
    and brings want. . . .

That calls in the night
    and dances on sunbeams,
that sings to a longing heart
    with silent tongue.

Can endless years keep
    the promises of yesterday?
What is the celestial light that
    defies darkness?

Is it love that entices
    with its mystic wand. . .
or only a dream that floats
    on heavenly clouds?

Fragment

Brightly lit,
it sits just inside the entrance,
like an ATM machine, but cashless,
offering only statistics to conjure old memories.

I decide to check it out later.

It is 2011, and I am a tourist at
the National War Memorial in Seoul,
a museum enshrining 5,000 years of Korean conflict,
where I can learn of ancient battles raging across centuries
by reading dry narratives and panoramas of pride and glory.

My interest perks up when the path leads to *our* Korean war.
I am reminded it began in 1950, before I was twelve:
    North rolling over South   US/UN rescuers in retreat
    Inchon landing turning the tide   MacArthur
    the Chinese   Truman   stalemate
and I recall a swirl of MovieTone news wrapped in patriotic music.

On the way out, I confront the memory machine,
gingerly tap   *English US New York*
then   *K-i-n-s*   . . . and up it comes:
"Sgt Harvey Kinsky, died April 23, 1953."

In an instant I see the face of Harvey,
my brother's buddy, who joined the Marines gung-ho
and was blown to bits three months before the shooting stopped.

They called him a hero back in 1953.

I never knew what they called my brother,
who got himself a "4-F" in the draft . . .
and stayed alive.

Wobbly

each step a test

clear pavement
conspires with
old ice lumps
to set insidious traps

slight twist of an ankle
awkward wiggle of a hip
arms wave like a high-wire walker

with constant fear of falling—galling,
while yet another runner imperturbably races by—

alien creatures with suction-cup feet?

oh no

just an army of young knee and hip muscles
perfectly coordinated
masterful on autopilot

ah youth

I keep walking old   slowly   slowly   attaboy!

The Struggle

In an era
of razor-sharp tongues
and fabricated facts

I believe
each episode of
racism
fear-mongering
random violence
blatant lying

intensifies
the prevalent wobble
of earth
on its axis

The ensuing cacophony
strives to stifle
those voices
pleading for the softness
of tolerance
reason and kindness

The world
holds its breath

Evening Ritual

Reminiscent of ant colonies
dispatched on mandatory marches,
we enthusiasts stream from dwellings,
drawn to a shore bejeweled with
glistening multi-colored shells.

A balmy, slightly salty onshore breeze
calms the Gulf of Mexico, welcomes
the arrivals. Some nestle in beach chairs.
Others seek preferred positions.
Cameras and eyes focus westward.
Excitement escalates.

The unfolding splendor grants us
license to momentarily suspend
earth's daily rotational relationship
with the sun. For this final act
we allege the sun is in motion
as it descends, splashes, then sets
into the watery horizon.

The disappearance of that final golden arc
elicits hugs, kisses, toasts and cheers.
We vow to congregate
for another Sanibel sunset,
as earth's rotation *resumes*.

Orpheus Pleads His Case

Already knowing love is a strong god
and that compassion is its advocate,
Orpheus began to plead with song
his strongest case to save Eurydice,
and to entreat what only hell can grant
and only what a lover's grief will risk.
Then Pluto sighed and looked with moistening eyes
for confirmation from his Proserpine
who was no longer a reluctant queen,
and now accustomed to the dark, she sensed
her husband's softened heart, so she advised
the king, her husband: "You should let them go,"
then qualifying through a slender smile,
"on one condition."

Sisyphus At the End of the Day

There was a certain heft and gradient
this day that made me think of you
once more and whether, Sisyphus, you thought
about the physics of your daily chore,
or (still better yet) you might just walk
away one day while leaving lie this load
in its own stasis at the mountain's base,
while shaking off the dust of hopelessness.
And this is when our similarities
begin to show: The truth is that you've come
to need this rock, its roughness and its weight
that scrapes your hands and arms and drains your will.
Our fate is not the whimsy of the gods,
but rather, the inertia of our minds.

Dudely May

Y'know, I'm into these lilac scents
and the birds that chirp and sing
before the dawn in trees along the fence—
it's a totally awesome thing.

My vibes become, like, optimum
when the May air stirs my pad—
I'm clueless where that rush comes from
but it's totally, totally rad.

I groove with the falling of way cool rain,
and I dig (oh, wow!) the space
of, like, thunderstorms (they fry my brain)
with subwoofer-quality bass.

Since the Dude laid down this happenin' season,
I'm thinking He must have meant it,
and if May should croak for any reason,
we'd have to, like, reinvent it.

Table Grace

We deeply offer our thanks
to the Deepest of Thankables
and our abiding love
to the Most Abiding of Lovables
as we gather here
in grace under grandness
humbly to eat of the earth
so that ripplings of renewal
may nurture and empower our
sweetly imperative lives.

May the sustenance we now
receive within ourselves
enable us to give out
more than we possess
as our lungs and souls
breathe more than is air
on our chosen journey
into more than we know.

We honor the One within us
while dwelling within the One.

Amen

Soul

Some use their souls to say there is no soul. Some use their
freedom to claim we are machines—denying what we know of
mystery. It is hard to tell which hell builds bigger walls to bar
eternity.

There's time to walk if we can't run. There's time for trees and
standing still. Eternity comes passing through, patiently as
sparrows do, singing pleasantly.

chilly equinox
coming cold or coming spring
sparrows bring new sound

Advent Darkness

This darkness isn't such that I
can brighten it by the light that I bring.
No laws of nature taint the sky.
No bonds bind it so it can't sing.

The power failed, but should we wait
for what might not come speedily?
Some of us would hesitate,
but darkness helps our hearts to see.

We're thankful for the light that's near.
Praise sound, but not with our ears solely.
Our voices stir the darkness here
repeating "Holy, Holy, Holy."

Paul Gaugin – Use of the Color Orange

When Paul Gaugin's work was at the Art Institute,
I was captivated by *Still Life with a Fan*,
amazed by his oranges, the bright fruit.
He used varnish so thick, it glowed very grand—
orange trees shown on a fan, so astute.
Paul, a prolific, endlessly creative man,
left Paris, where he had his roots,
under the peace treaty with Japan.
The *Fire Dance* has fire that shoots
high above trees like magic crayons.
People gather around the flames, ever mute,
as they gaze at the fire without any plans.
Gaugin was most known for Tahiti,
bright orange colors, and long-lost deities.

A Warning to Pain

"Pain can only feed on pain. Pain cannot feed
on joy. It finds it quite indigestible." —Eckhart Tolle

I will not feed you tasty tidbits
of ripened succulent sadness
nor any juicy morsels
stuffed with loss of hope.

Never will I present to you a plate
piled high with tender aches and anguish
nor serve to you a sumptuous meal
of my despair, lest you swell
with misplaced pride.

I will not place in front of you
a bowl of deep discouragement
or savory stew of thickened grief.
And do not think you will grow strong
by ever feasting in my fields of sorrow.

Oh no—let me be clear,
for in the coming days as I watch
you wither and waste away,
I will feed you only endless joy—
in hopes that you may choke on it.

Movements at Dusk

The window measures two feet
by six—just right to create
a Zen view. I shift position
on the sofa to reframe it as though
taking a photograph. Aiming for
asymmetrical balance, an instinct
honed years ago in Doug Gilbert's
photography class, I place the trunk
of the linden tree off-center,
balancing it with two slivers of light
still lingering from the low-slung
evening sun of late June.

I absorb the notes flowing
from the seven-foot Bosendorfer—
my husband playing Chopin—
one of the fifty-eight mazurkas,
a form the composer kept
coming back to, over the course
of his short thirty-nine years, pieces
graced with the lilt of Polish dances,
gentle echoes of his childhood.

Beyond the window, linden leaves
shift in time to the music,
branches stretch their fingers
as melodies drift from the piano.

With no prelude a light show begins
beneath the tree's canopy.
Pinpoints of light blaze
for less than a second, flicker
and flash back into darkness.

Random locations randomly lit—
tonight the fireflies dance the mazurka.

WWII Warren, Indiana

German prisoners of war
Are coming to our farm?
Daddy tells us, *Yes, it's true,*
Carl Simpson's canning factory
over in Plum Tree is leasing a field
from us to grow tomatoes that
the prisoners will help farm.

Are they bad men?
Will they hurt us?
Daddy tells us, *There will be*
soldiers as guards. We will be safe.

Where will they live?
Daddy tells us, *There is a prison tent*
camp in Eaton, and a bus will
bring them to the farm every day.

They come when the tomato plants
are tall enough to weed.
From the window we see the men
getting off the bus.
Mommy, they look just like us.

Later Daddy walks down to the field
to see what is happening.
Daddy tells the guards,
They are pulling the tomato plants
and leaving the ragweed.

They don't understand,
came the reply.
Daddy believes differently.

back by the barn

hollyhocks
grow tall at the back
of our garden against
the old barn beside
the dill weed that Mom uses
for her pickles

we girls make dolls
from their dainty flowers
fairy sprites in
pink and white tutus
dancing in our summer garden

rhubarb
comes up every year
in front of the hollyhocks,
its green leaves—that
Dad warns us are poison—
seem as big as the ears on
circus elephants that
come to town in July

Grandma calls it pie plant
when she bakes her yummy pies
but I love best to chew the shiny red
puckeringly sour stalks as I play
with my dolls back by the barn

Often-Used Clichés from My 1940s Childhood

A little bird told me "Don't step on that crack,
the world is your oyster, don't break your mom's back."
You're a sight for sore eyes, but Thomas is doubtful
and Charlie's a horse with a milk-toasty snout-full.
Sure, Jack's a dull boy, but he's great at all trades.
Say "Robinson" quickly, you'll win points in spades.
Bark up the wrong tree. Buy a pig in a poke.
You'll be mad as a hatter, and maybe dead broke.

At sixes and sevens, we're babes in the wood
with our Ps and Qs minded and manners quite good.
By gosh and by golly, by hook or by crook,
"snug as a bug" is the best phrase, in my book.
As slow as molasses, as quiet as a mouse,
if you eat too much cake, you'll be big as a house.
Hold on to your horses. Falls hurt like the dickens.
Keep your upper lip stiff if you find there's slim pickin's.
While kits and caboodles lift you high on the hog,
the cookie still crumbles, and the tail wags the dog.

When the devil is hindmost you can talk willy-nilly,
then lickety-split you begin to sound silly.
A flibberty-gibbet complains—okie-doke
but hicketty-picketty's tricks are no joke.
Now out of the bag comes a cat that's meowing
and my tongue from that frog in my throat is bow-wowing.
The lamb's tail is shaking—I'm not sure just why,
but to cut off his nose would produce a loud cry.
Like the pot yelling "black" and the kettle complaining
when we bury the hatchet, cats and dogs begin raining.

That's my tale in a nutshell. You may want me to squirm,
but our early bird's happy, he's eaten his worm.
This chip off the block now waits with breath bated,
just a drop in the bucket among clichés backdated.

Swiss Traveling Troop
Based on Cole Porter's "We Open in Venice" *from* Kiss Me Kate

We open in Zermatt. Our next stop is Davos.
From Flims on to Wengen (lots of rosti in Wengen!).
Our next stop is Klosters, then Lenk and Pontresina
then Appenzell and Engleberg, then we open again, Where?

We climb to Mannlichen and gaze at the Eiger
cross Diavolezza (lots of ice in that glacier!).
We climb to Sunnega then Hunderwilerhohe
then Riffelalp and Fuhrenalp, then we open again, Where?

On free days we travel to Lucerne and Montreux
then on through Graubunden (lots of brats in Graubunden!)
to Chur and Schaffhusen, Kleine Sheidegg and St. Gallen
then Unterwalden, Oberwald, then we open again, Where?

We hop on the post bus, line up for the Metschbahn.
We take the cog railway (lots of cogs in this railway!).
On chair lifts and coaches, express trains and more bahnen,
funiculars and cable cars, then we open again, Where?

We take photos of forests and hang-gliding trip mates,
of cows dressed in flowers (lots of cows wearing flowers!).
We cross lakes and rivers: the Aa, the Rhine, the Simmen,
the Bodensee, the Thunersee, then we open again, Where?

Berg Fuhrer retires. He'll no longer lead us.
We don't want to end it. (There's joy in those mountains!)
For our final reunion, we'll visit our great favorites.
We'll reminisce, then that is it. We'll reunite, Where?

In Heaven!

Fall

Fall leaves
    float without a sound
Acorns
    drop quickly to the ground
Milkweed pods
    burst open wide
Wooly bears
    cross roads from each side
Geese
    fill the autumn sky
Monarchs
    either fly or they die

Light As a Feather

True Love
light as a feather
soft as a kitten
gentle as a breeze.

True Love
makes you kinder
so much better
strong as an oak.

True Love
floats across you
lifts you skyward
on its own breeze.

Prince Charming

One warm summer evening I sat
on my patio, feet propped up,
book in hand, Max and Princess
lazing nearby—when a toad hopped out.

Not wishing to intrude,
he chose a brick near the edge,
not too close, not too far. He sat.
An outsider.

Imperious, like an old Dowager Duchess,
Princess lifted her head,
stared down at the interloper,
then at Max. Duty called.

Max rose, approached the toad,
circled several times, cautious,
and nudged it with his nose.
Steadfast, the toad sat.

To send a loud, clear masculine message
Max lifted his hind right leg and sprinkled.
The toad blinked his large eyes, unmoved.
Unchallenged, Max resettled near Princess,
satisfied his women were safe.

Night after night, we four sat—
Max and Princess at my feet,
our toad on his favorite brick,
me with a book. The summer
we chose to share a setting sun.

daffodils
tall yellow soldiers
stand at attention

a hummingbird
sips nectar from the feeder
splendor flits away

scissor tails
streak across dawn's orange sky
greeting morning's sun

All These Things
For our Mom
"Dolores"

All the state-of-the-art medical equipment
All the medications and home health visits
All the meals we cooked and ate together
All the naps taken on Sunday afternoons
All the visits from friends and neighbors
All the church going and soul searching
All the special food, the shopping trips
All the meowing from Baby and Dolly
All the love we pressed into her hands
All the hospitals, and there were four
All the care and concern we gave her
All the time spent in hospital rooms
All the trust we had for technology
All the days since her first surgery
All the prayers for her well-being
All the questions for every doctor
All the times we cried out in fear
All the times we said I love you
All the doctors and surgeons
All the fun we had together
All the talking and sharing
All the laughs we shared
All the plans we made
All the hope we felt
All of the hugs
All the tears
Could not
Save
Her

Pernicious Visitor

I can't see it but I know it's there.
I know its painful touch
barging into my body, my life,
destroying my plans,
gripping my lively existence,
twisting it into—this.
Do I fight or accept it?
I must do both; they go hand in hand;
although I don't have time for either,
and yet time becomes the issue.
Time is now spent taking shots, pills, and poison
to deceive, to destroy the growing evil,
and all the time it eats and eats.

What can I do? I'll do it!
What can I say? I'll say it!
If I run away, it comes with me.
Even if I shut down, it never sleeps.
I must live one step ahead
of the clutches lurking within me,
and all the time it eats and eats.

And there is only so much time, after all.
I gaze at the faces of loved ones.
Their eyes fall to the floor,
hoping against hope.
They know my fight and wait with me
to see if I will surmount or succumb.
I resolve to surmount.
I just hope my body listens.
It works overtime to fight and fight.
So tired, yet I must stay strong,
afraid it will overtake me in a weak moment,
and all the time it eats, and eats, and eats.

Stripped-Down Clown

Eyebrows and lips
sit on top of cotton
their secret guarded
by a plastic bag
only the clean-up crew
can access.

Boxed storage
holds the breath of
red hair
round nose
and oversized floppy white shoes
in wait for their next appearance.

Layers of charm and cheer
wit and giggles
peel away to
streaks of white face
red, yellow, and blue costume.
The last props to be shed
before the reality of flesh
adopts a new personality
that leaves
the smell of popcorn
and cotton candy
the sound of children's laughter
ferocious lion roars
the colorful residue of happiness
and entertainment
behind a darkened tent flap.

Daisy Run Over by Tricycle

Does he love me
does he not
smashed
soul ripped
across coarse cement
pushed into a superstitious crack.
Wafting scent
of dragging disappointment
sweet
fresh
yellow slaughtered fragrance.
Final surge
stripped white petals
blown off to heaven
as the street lights signal
it's time to go home.

Sisyphus Discusses Writing Poetry
During an Interview with the
Athens Free Press on His Day Off

It's an effort to translate
heart throb and heartbreaks
gunfire and Gandhi
maternity wards and hospices
into different tangibilities,
into words the
cortex and auditory system
can convert to
things from feelings.

And it's all academic.
I just write historical mysteries:
Who did What with Which,
and to Whom.
I'm merely a cartographer,
describing what I saw
before the earth moved again.
Here were monsters
cloaked as memories.

IED QED

Depleted uranium
is still on the Periodic Table.
It waits there for you
or you can search if you feel prompted.
The tap of your fingers will seem a sudden
        silence
as the sun sets.

Zep's "Stairway" issues from the boom box.
Above and beyond you at the fifty,
the New Guy screams along, off key.
You holler something to him
and miss the signal from the sensor.
The shell was stolen from a stockpile.
It took four men to hide it in your path.

Even as I run from my truck to yours
I know there's no reason to hurry.
Heavy metal thunder echoes from the hills.
There's screaming but no climbing notes to match.
Your dog tags, wrapped like mourning bands for
        silence,
weigh more than worlds upon my palm.

A Las Vegas Story

Coming out from the smoky casino
after losing his shirt
the old man with bloodshot eyes
was thrilled to find
the setting sun
brilliant and round
on the horizon

eagerly he grasped his last chip
and threw it
into the black hole
of the universe.

Good Medicine

in herbal medicine
bitter is better

yet as a poet
I find just the opposite

a gentle breeze
a sweet chirp
a blooming flower
a green leaf
an innocent smile
a lively melody

especially

a good poem a day
keeps the doctor away

No Good Deed and All That Jazz

On my whizzing winter walk to Union Station
I'd pop change into her jingle box.
Money for the homeless!" she'd shriek,
her voice rough by 7:30 a.m.

At her spot on Chicago River's bridge at Jackson,
her right hand rattled the container's contents,
one arm flailing out to passersby.
Her grey cloth coat clutched at the collar,
holey grey gloves, some fingers missing,
white hair tucked into a knit cap, face etched.

One morning, I had no money
to slip through her box's slit top.
My eyes smiled an apology.
Never had there been a thank you before—
just an extra jingle thrust
as her unblinking eyes pierced through the cold,
her straight lips shrieked out
to the next person walking behind me.

She beckoned me to come near,
bumping her box at me, a wry smile.
Did she recognize me after so many months?
"My apologies. Today I don't have any. . . ."
She leaned toward me, her stare demonic,
and spat at my fur hat.

Looking Out the Back Door
of Jackie B's Laundromat

Metra train pulls into
the station and
commuters leak out.

Raising painted umbrellas,
they drift across the ponding parking lot
like Monet's water lilies,
scattering in different directions.

I soak up the stillness,
waiting for my dollar's worth
of drying time to end.

Opioid Blues

Addicts are decorated kites.
Cut loose the string,
they drift away
and land in a different yard.

I miss his
burning colors
tickling the sky.

Nightmare: A Snake Poem
We talk with goblins, owls and sprites:
If we obey them not, this will ensue,
They'll suck our breath, or pinch us black and blue.
--Dromio of Syracuse, The Comedy of Errors, *Act 2, Scene 1*

Not dark woods, but the city's heart, **we**
wander, fearful, almost hesitant to **talk**.
The moon hides behind clouds. **With** trepidation,
we tread on shadows, hear **goblins** groan
and growl. In a tree three **owls** give hellish hoots,
call out our names, **and** seek to lead us on. Through
fog we see six **sprites** who tempt us to forget
our destination. **If** we follow, their magic
will control. **We** ponder where to go
and whether to **obey** our own instincts
or follow **them** wherever they lead. We turn
away but **not** in time; invisible cords
pull us **this** way and that. We cannot
do what we **will**, but only what they force us to.
What will **ensue**? Owls hoot again, the goblins groan.
Now **they'll** hold us captive. Like children
we **suck** our thumbs for comfort,
wish for **our** friends to come and save us.
We feel the **breath** of ghouls hot against our skin.
Will they kill us **or** enslave us? Are we in
a dream? I **pinch** myself to see, but it seems real.
They hold **us** captive. Streetlights blink out.
All is **black** until we reach out to each other
and hold hands. Sprites disappear. The sky
turns **blue**.

Grandmother's Bread

When I asked Grandmother how to bake bread,
she said put on an apron, gather the ingredients.

Roll up your sleeves. Pour out a mound of flour,
she said. Make a valley in the white mountain
and plant yeast. Let a little salt snow fall.
Make streams of egg white and melted butter flow
before plopping down golden yolk suns.

Let your fingers press and turn, mix and knead,
turn and fold, knead and turn to the rhythm
of your life till it feels right. Roll it into a ball
round as the earth. Cover with a flour-sack towel.

Preheat the oven, grease the pans. Let the dough
rest while you sit with hot coffee and a neighbor.
Let the leaven have its way with friendship and dough.

Push the dough back down, press as life presses you
and your neighbor whose husband drinks too much.
Fold and knead, turn and fold, till it's ready to grow.

Break and roll it into loaves. Put them into pans
and into the oven. In half an hour, pull out golden loaves.
Slice one hot, serve with honey-butter and fresh coffee
to that friend who craves bread, who needs something
sweet to get her through another day.

October in Vermont

A post-breakfast walk
before mercurial rain
takes me up the road

past the farm's
rolling land embraced
by folded mountains

walling in the little town
below. Fading leaves
hang motionless

in a quietude nothing
disturbs but my footsteps
and breathing.

It's harder to describe
the tender mew
and gurgle of a stream

purling toward the river
pulsing each day with its
own rhythm and secrets

that flow to a watershed
where each droplet's
outcome is assured.

Lesson From the Mountains

Sometimes the path grows steep
and the air slices into thinning doubt
but you keep walking
past bitter stones of hope.

A crescent moon competes
with shimmering sun
that washes over resilient granite
like an urgent call

to unwrap the fortitude saved
for sudden barbed winds
that splinter your heart
like the white bones of dead trees.

Golden flames of light
exhaled by autumn aspens
reminding you to crack open
crystals of courage

on your halfway to somewhere,
each bite of translucent sky
big enough to swallow
all fear.

Drawing of My Kindergarten Boyfriend
as Shetland Pony

Nicker me
stomp your hooves against
cafeteria table
split your PB&J in two
give me half
Make Solomon proud

Handiwork

I am the one driving across the Rust
Belt but it is my mother's hands attached
to my wrists, planted at 10 & 2.
Liver spots skim across the crepe
paper skin, while gnarly knuckles prop
up the dorsal flesh like Boy Scout pup
tents across Nebraska.

The narrow gold band spins loose.
It might still be mine
but the wearing thin is all her,
just a matter of time before it breaks away.

I catch my reflection in the rear view
mirror, my head shimmers, a mess of crucified
bobby pins. A triangular piece of chiffon
to knot under my chin cannot be far off.

Only my fingernails are unchanged.
Her emphysemic clubbing is AWOL.
My own short, flat nails remain. I never loved
the fags like my WAC of a mother.

The Answer

I pray over broken wings,
  scattered petals,
    and lost feathers.
I seek messages
  in splashing fountains,
    pools of rain and
      shallow streams.
Darkened clouds,
  rain drops
    and snow flakes
      speak to me.
I hear voices in the
  chorus of thunderclaps
    and raging winds.
I study the walls
  of cave dwellers
    looking for messages
      and signs.
Every voice I hear,
  each wing, petal,
    feather and star
      is your creation.

The pounding ocean thunders,
        I AM.
I whisper,
        I know.

Solstice

Now the pale leaf unfurls itself to green,
and pink has settled on the budded rose.
The brown thrush heralds all he knows of spring,
and hummingbirds feel stirrings that they know.

Wind in petal-laden boughs plucks at the harp
of magnolias housing nightingale's sweet song.
An early frost warns finches, turning sharp—
again we know that winter stayed too long.

The stream of winter's tears flows from the gate,
full of petals torn from heightened boughs.
Will we remember all of their bright fate
and celebrate not why they left, but how?

Oh! Can we learn to love a spring that's late
or love a winter going into June?
Or like a summer evening when its fate
is ended by the light of harvest moon?

We will accept untimely gifts of grace;
a November rose in bloom smells just as sweet,
and thank the God who brought us to this place,
for the winter that we know is now complete.

Pentecost
The Royal Botanical Gardens, Madrid

The irises today speak in tongues,
their little beards bristling
in the mottled light.

Not yet! It's barely Easter.
The day of the Spirit
has not yet come! But flowers
are oblivious. They have crouched
far too long in the stone-cold ground,
and on this first warm day
of crepuscular gladness,

they have gathered themselves
in the upper room of the garden,
riding in on their own ruffled wings,
their dark fiery bodies singing
silent alleluias.

After the Solstice

Every day, more light, they say, and yet
sky smothers earth like an old pillow.
Squirrels hide in clumps of leftover leaves.
Trees inscribe eternal winter on the roofs.
We huddle indoors, remembering

past winters, old holidays, and all those
who look down on us from the violet
dusk of heaven. We seek comfort
in blankets, hot tea, television shows
from another generation. The world

is a color impossible to paint,
a music soundless, without fanfare.
Night still settles in early, leaving
ebony footprints in the drifted snow,
backing off one step at a time. Meanwhile,

I am drugged with the expectation
of lilacs in bud and robins nesting again
in the eaves. But for now,
the cold is my epiphany
and darkness my star.

Ballena Vallarta

The humpback whale and her calf
appear to swim in our ocean of air,
their sculpted fins touching in perfect
equilibrium above a base of bronze.

I admire their stayed movement, this
posed ballet between whale and calf,
this example of tender mother-love
that the sculptor has created of metal.

I close my eyes and try to recall the first
ocean I swam in, try to feel the tug of
the umbilical cord that once anchored
me, try to remember my mother's touch.

Found

A pair of matching men's hair brushes
in sterling silver with the monogramed
letters FRJ engraved on the top of each
one; this pair of Art Nouveau men's hair
brushes with stiff black bristles embedded
in wood bases; these discarded sterling
silver hair brushes that I found in a pile
of trash along with someone's old letters
and family pictures; hair brushes that now
sit on my bedroom bureau to remind me
of my father's brushes mother threw away
when she remarried.

Emma

they marched
in many cities
80 by 10,000
in D.C. alone
filling streets
and parkland
with mostly
faces of our
kids under 20
shouting enough
is enough no more
no more school shootings
no more guns our soldiers
use in war and battlefields
speeches filled with anger
speeches filled with pain
speeches filled with loss
but one girl read off the
names of recent victims
then stood silently
six and a half minutes
until an alarm sounded
the time it took for 17
to die to be killed by bullets
her silence was a moment
heard all around the world
I heard you EMMA

Affirmation

At sixty-four there is more
but since age seven
I've awaited my death—
at Uncle Joe's funeral
I learned *we all die.*

My mother did not ask me
to kiss his corpse. What relief
to stand in the twilight alone
with God yet with my family
in a slanted room full of shadows,

to be thankful for my mother's mercies
yet frightened by my grandma's tears
for her brother and to stare at it
pale and coldly stern in a box
and wonder why I am alive and here now.

Yes!

That was
the spring when
Hope hid so well
some feared that she was
dead or fled forever
to a more deserving realm.
Signs
      were
          not
              good—
black buds, cold dry rot.
Yet now and then
a bird's call
broke the
spell.

Phase Change

Once upon a
heartbeat
      wing-flash
          petal drop
our eyes meet
for the very first time.
Silent tree leans
toward sun-splashed
earth, past the tipping point.
Gloriously slow,
stout limbs
hit the ground and
shatter, learn to leap.

Snowflakes kiss
the bloom and melt
on contact, or with
breathless stealth in
agonizing, exquisite dis-
integration—
all a point of view.
Frost ferns form
on window glass,
star tracks
scratch the night.

We are nine-
tenths water,
born of the sea,
reborn to the sky.

Slow motion fast forward
looking back
here and now and
there and everywhere....

Photo Op, Early Evening

A great blue heron, the first I've seen all year,
stands on a half-submerged log in the preserve's
four-acre pond.

A visitor raises her cell phone to photograph the
bird. She yells at him, tries to make him fly. The bird
is unmoved—a Zen monk waiting for a new moon.

The woman commands her husband and son to pick up
rocks to throw at the heron, make him flap away, but
the rocks fall short. "Throw harder," she yells.

The boy slips in the water, loses his balance. The father
wades in, rescues his son while the mother captures it all
on her cell.

the great blue heron
master of immense quiet
a blue moon at dusk

Find me

in some lost anthology
the library forgot
to remainder,
or in a chapbook
gifted by an eccentric aunt.

Find me
on my special page.
Read me out loud.
Press your fingers
on your throat.

Feel our pulse.

Learn my words by heart.
Share them with your
closest friends.

Tell readers that these
words are our blood
in the flow of life

in mortality.

The Long and Rolling Flow

If I close my eyes, I see the Ohio River
winding its way, a long ribbon of silver.
I remember fish markets along the bank,
anchored on water, connected by a plank.
I smell the rich odor: muddy water and fish.
I love the fried catfish Mom puts on my dish.
The power of my memories is like a freight train,
grips me so strong it's hard to explain.

Riding the river ferry on its crooked way
to the other side is like a slow, watery ballet.
I hear a whippoorwill call in the night, it
echoes across the Ohio, much to my delight.
Little brother and I play in the shallow waters,
splashing with glee, two young river otters.
Back and forth, back and forth the jet boats fly,
pull water skiers on a hot, sunny 4th of July.
Towering bluffs above the shadowed river,
witness its history as the great survivor.

As river barges silently navigate along,
carry precious cargo, cruising so very strong,
I recall Dad's stories of life on the Ohio River, in
the faint misty music of his old violin.

This is my parable of the Ohio River so long ago.
I do so want to see again its long and rolling flow.

Collarless in Athens
To the street dogs and all who care for them

Climb the hill to the Acropolis
before midday. Admire the view:
pearl-grey clouds that gather
above lavender mountains, glassy sea,
the classical columns of cut marble

against an aquamarine sky. Hear
gulls screech and scold overhead.
Watch the Greek flag pulse on pole
in wind as tourists scramble across
rocks worn smooth over millennia

by ancient sandals, modern Nikes,
in tribute to the virgin goddess
of victory, Athena. Listen to the stones
for residual prayer offered up by rulers
and priests since Neolithic times.

Look close, peer into the shadows—
there you will find a yellow street dog
resting in the shade of an olive tree,
oblivious to the noisy, bustling herd
of humanity who push past, like me,

pause long enough to pose for snapshots,
selfies with iPhones, iPads, before hustling
back to tour buses. Observe the people
who get too close, like the bluebottles
buzzing nearby. See the yellow dog

look up, sniff the air, indifferent
as he shifts position, naps. Marvel
at this lowly stray, anointed
keeper of the path into the temple.

Headscarves & Tiaras
after Jack Ridi

It is said that the Queen's corgis
are Britain's most privileged pooches—
they feast from silver salvers, dine
on the choicest lamb or rabbit, the freshest
veggies from Elizabeth II's own table
(no kibble ever touches their lips!).

Say yes to wanting to be one of her pack—
you'll live in luxury, slumber on satin pillows
in wicker baskets elevated to avoid the draughts
at Windsor, Balmoral & Buckingham Palace.
You'll travel first class in chauffeur-driven
limos, airplanes & helicopters. You are
carried down steps by aides & footmen.
You'll roam freely & sometimes run amok.

You have been known to interrupt meetings
with foreign dignitaries, annoy visitors
at garden fêtes, nip the ankles of postmen.
You'll sulk when Her Majesty wears a tiara,
but leap into action when she dons a headscarf,
bark & rush madly to the nearest door.
You won't know that the squirrels don't exist
for you. You won't ever worry about money,
illness or death. You will wag your tail.

Lament for Summer's End

Morning so still the crickets hold their trill,
a pheasant far away calls and retreats,
the sun slides between clouds and reappears
in early chill.

Late-summer as it is, there is a chill
that warns of days to come: the fallen leaves
crackle weeks early, blowing in light wind
down every hill.

We look to see fall colors on the hill
where only August dusty-green presides.
All roadside flowers take on stronger hues
as if to fill

the void now making. What delight can fill
our senses when the colors fade and birds
are flown to warmer lands? We learn to dread
morning so still.

Light Moves with a Circular Motion

The hoop rolls down the walk—
circle on a line, dark against white,
childhood over and over.

After four weeks of dark, darker—
then more and more light:
the moon is a circle again,
pale and sensuous as a gauze-veiled breast.

Sharp angled lines
bisect a chalked circle;
the geometry class disputes
a difficult theorem.

He gives her a ring, says his endless love
will circle her days if she accepts it.

In a black circle on grey ground
thirteen hooded figures
weave intricate harmonics.
Each casts over her shoulder
a dead leaf from an enchanted tree.
Each steps three times around
the center shrine.

Empty wineglasses
leave white-circled reminders;
on a phonograph a forgotten record
turns   turns   turns.

Falling leaves,
snowfall, blossom scatter,
and the weight of sun
complete another circle
of the pinwheel of seasons.

Climate Change

It has been a bipolar spring,
one day hot, the next cold.
It has left me
and the whole world wondering
how to manage comfort
for the next 24 hours.
Tentative foliage
resists strong wind
fluffing it out.
Days of standing still
rather than the gradual growth
of myriad green occur.
Then amid faint pastel cool days
comes a very warm day.
Out pop sudden, brilliant
fruit blossoms and light-filled,
deep-colored tulip cups.
The bright days hurt
my eyes and my heart
with their beauty.
The grey, cold juxtaposition
of the next day
causes me to wonder
if what I know of seasons
can be trusted.

The Deal

There is always
a negotiation
when one offers
to help another.
How great is the need?
How much is the cost
to the one giving
and to the one receiving?
What is the known
or unknown transaction
taking place?
Who will benefit?
One or the other
or both?
Or, is it a deal
for the good
of the Universe,
a breath-taking gift
of greatness of heart?

Stormy Night

I can hear
Thunder rolling
In the moonless dark night
Zigzag lightning
Winds getting sarcastic
Trees shaking
Leaves flying out
Saying goodbye to their trees
And then gently settling down
On the ground
Chipmunks murmuring
Time for tea
Time for tea

I make sure
All is safe
And sound inside
I pray for well-being
Of everyone everywhere
On this turbulent night

Pomegranate

Bright red
and beautiful,
a delicious fruit
from heaven,
mentioned in the holy books

Its fabulous creation
ruby-like beauty
within the layers
appears as honeycomb

Nature's jewels—
juicy sweet little seeds
spurt zest
into our mouths

A food for longevity
full of fiber, antioxidants
and vitamins,
healing mankind
for ages

Oedipus Complains

The gods are *just*. Okay, so
couldn't they sound a warning?
Why is it that one morning
we wake to find our pleasant vice
hung rotting round our necks,
the piper waiting in the doorway
to collect his price?
It seems a paltry way
to repay us for being merely human.
Merely human? I mean completely human:
devoutly, wildly, willfully human.
We've played our part of the game
and counted not the cost;
the rules there don't seem to be the same,
and just as we begin to learn them, we've lost.

Will There Be Music After Death?

The question sometimes bothers me, because
no tune I've learned within our human laws
seems likely to last longer than my breath.
It's hard to think that when my ears are done—
these fragile flaps of skin and tympanum—
there will be anything for sound to sound upon.
Who can strike rhythm from a broken drum?
And if there is no song, what signifies
that metaphoric horde of harping angels,
those cherubs plucking lute and psaltery?
That unseen choir makes us falter; we
can't imagine sounds we do not hear.
Stretching to peg their drift, we tend to fear
that we may tune our string of faith too far.
But maybe music is mere metaphor—
not what our hearing is intended for,
but what is fashioned for our hearing's aid,
so we can apprehend what we can't see.
And in the hour of music's dissolution,
our strings unstrung, reeds riddled, stops unstopped,
we shall leave melody and find its Source—
then Sound, unbounded from the chords of time,
shall flow through us, round us in a timeless course.
No need to hear the Goldberg variations when
we're the theme toward which their pattern tends.

Once in a While

The alarm didn't end your dream.
You uncurl, roll over, and stretch.
Half-past nine and you have no plans:
no meetings, no appointments,
no friend turning twenty-nine today,
no calls to make or emails to send.
The Keurig beckons from below
with the promise of vanilla or hazelnut,
as you reflect on nothing in particular.

If you wish, you can peek at the personals,
maybe rise and watch a morning talk show,
even start that Irish short story.
A top-down drive is tempting.
It's seventy and sunny with only
a soft breeze brushing the trees, but
the pillow maintains a gentle hold of
your head, whispers temptingly that
just today, you might lie around
a bit longer, if you like.

Once in a while, life can go on
without you playing your daily part.

Old Couples at Siesta Key

As the sea swallows the western sun,
old couples leave soft, firm footprints
in the feathery white sands of Siesta Key.

Some walk hand in hand or arm in arm,
while others, though not touching,
are held tight by unbreakable cords.

Their pace is slow, yet certain, a
calm steadiness in their gait, forged
by years of traveling as one.

At times, young lovers make light
with a wistful, "Us in fifty, honey,"
hoping it's true, behind their giggles.

Now and then, the walkers stare seaward,
perhaps wondering, as their days wind down,
just why we live and love and must leave.

But as they look out and ponder the horizon,
it is they who give answer to the sea
by their presence on the shore.

Stuck

When you get stuck, it's like an act of fate:
stuck in traffic, gearshift stuck in third,
or stuck in an elevator, where you wait
for hours on end before your cries are heard.
The job you started twenty years ago
to tide you over for a month or two
has given you insurance, HMO,
yet doesn't help with bills marked *Overdue*.
You're stuck with coaching Jenny's soccer team,
and later on, as football referee.
The in-laws pull you toward a business scheme
that's nothing more than hope and *bonhomie*.
Yet fate held sway, and Cupid played his part
by having you get stuck inside my heart.

The Gravedigger

His tools rest against
the hundred-year-old cemetery wall.
His rough stone cottage in shadow—
three rooms, window frames distressed.
So knifing, the cold this winter.

Too many deaths
and the ground is frozen.
He fears his lopsided
shoulder won't last
another digging.

Calloused hands, liver hardened
from liquor he gulps
throughout the day and night.
He stares from behind curtains
at sobbing mourners,
imagines how they'll carry on
if his work satisfies.

His raspy cough grates the night
and his sleep is turbulent from tremors.
On his donated, twin bed
his closed eyelids
close nothing out.

He dreams of mourners,
of stony ground
and ill-made coffins
given to the poor.
He wonders who will dig
his grave, and how soon.

Tunnel Rat

Head-first into the hole
no wider than his shoulders,
the tunnel rat kicked the air and disappeared
into subterranean bowels of possible doom.
Viet Cong booby traps awaited him,
ready to ignite into a billion broken stars.
Meticulous spiders mended the dark, dank air.
Impatient scorpions and cunning vermin scurried about.

But the tunnel rat pressed on,
moved like a blind fish
easing towards imagined blue.
He questioned each root, twig, and rock
within the gold ring his flashlight cast before him.
Through silver lice, shit, maggots, and vapor of pestilence,
the smallest man in the platoon crawled furiously on,
tunneled past death stacked into blind corners,
left strips of his flesh,
clutched the mission to make it home
as tightly as he gripped his 45.

cashier says
he has a lovely smile—
shooting stars

dependent on a tangled rainbow—
EKG cables

under makeup
beyond the reach of talk
her scars

email fist bump —
a friend's wife
joins him for lunch

lawn care noise
with cicada hum—
late summer harmony

dinner table
at the commune—
the flies nobody swats

a thank-you letter
from the eye bank;
dark afternoon

cattle train
my sons clamor
for Big Mac

moonlit granite…
I wait for the bear
to circle back

moonrise
i give up trying
to tie it down

overnight snow
the feral cat's tracks
reveal a sixth toe

I Love a Monday

The squeaky swing next door
hangs static on its chain.
A tricycle sits on the driveway
parked at a forlorn angle
its daredevil driver ferried away
on a yellow school bus
with others of his ilk
and their exhausting vitality.

A brown beer bottle
not done partying
tips itself over the rim
of a trash bin
rolls drunkenly to the curb
comes to rest in the gutter.

The usual barking dogs
sleep off a weekend's excitement.
A tea bag steeps silently
in a porcelain pot, its spout chipped
by some careless ancestor.

The only sounds I record are
the sigh of an old cottonwood
and the distant hum of suburban commerce.
It is so quiet I could hear the sound
of pen on paper if only the pen would
stop scratching the back of my head
or twirling like a mini baton
through impatient fingers.

If the blue-inked fine point
pen would cooperate
you might know how happy
and productive I am
on a Monday.

Kabul Dead End

A woman stands alone
covered head turned
to a crumbling wall
shoulders hunched
protecting a secret.
She takes something
from a drab cloth bag
maybe a cell phone
for a forbidden call
or a knife
weapon of honor
in defense or revenge
or, even more dangerous,
a book of poetry.

At the Dollar Store

This shabby-looking guy walks up and says,
   You look familiar.
I inch back, start to glance away.
   I know you, he says.
He's too close! He's in my space!
I'm planning my next move when,
   You know, from the shelter.
   You work at the homeless shelter, don't you?
I'm still taken aback, but I know now what he means.
   You served me breakfast.
Suddenly my stiffness begins to melt away. "Oh yes, I remember."
   I never forget a face, he says.
How can he remember me? I don't remember him.
I quickly construct a polite question. "So, how are things going?"
   Pretty good,
            I do my best
                  and the rest is up to God.
I search for a few profound words, but my brain is mush.
I say nothing. He extends his hand.
   I'm John.
"Pleased to meet you, John," I say, as we shake.

Half Way Up the Mountain
I feel for those with less,
I feel for those with more.

From my perch half way up the mountain,
I can see the very peak,
I can look down and see the foothills at the base.

The bottom can't be seen by those at the top.
Many up there have no concept
the bottom even exists.

Some arrive at the top
after a long, arduous climb,
others are born there.

Days at the top are spent amassing more and more,
worried they will lose what they have,
struggling to maintain their footing on the slippery slopes.

Those at the base search for a foothold,
a pathway up the mountain.
Many languish in repeated failure,
unable to climb very far before being stymied,
forced to try a different trail.

Some try hard,
others don't try at all.
Some are successful;
a few haven't the tools to even begin.

From my perch half way up the mountain
I watch climbers trekking by.
Those seeking wealth nod and stay their course.
Those seeking happiness rest here a while
. . . and for some reason never seem to leave.

Game Makers

Whatever happened
to boys with bats
in hand becoming
Stan the Man?

After gathering
at a playground
they'd make rules
and boundaries

For big leaguers
playing "left field"
or "Indian Ball"

With adults
being involved
not at all

Fit for Print

Newspapers
for all seasons
bit the dust

When cell phones
and iPads
took the touch

From persons
wanting to grab
the news

Now seen
on a screen
or other tool

Making readers
care less about
what once
was a must

Acknowledgments

Previously published poems include the following:

Jocelyn Ajami, "rubble," Second Prize 22nd International Kusamakura Haiku Competition, *Prize-Winning Haiku Magazine*, Kumamoto, Japan, 2018

Susan B. Auld, "crocus bloom," "still summer air," *Chrysanthemum* 22/October 2017; "black birds," *Autumn Moon* Volume 1:1 Winter 2017-2018; "unpacking," *Frogpond* 41:1; "empty of clouds," *Acorn*, Fall 2017; "shaping," *Heron's Nest,* Volume XVIII #3, September 2016

E. Izabelle Cassandra Alexander, "Maria's Broken Heart," *The International Who's Who in Poetry* Anthology 2005

Sherri Lohrum Baker, "Forever Autumn," Illinoispoets.org 2016

Mary Jo Balistreri, "Wedding," *Contemporary Haibun online* 2016; "At Saylesville Pond," *a hundred gourds,* British Haiku Society 2014

Camille A. Balla, "Autumn-Kissed," *St. Anthony Messenger* 2007, *Simple Awakenings* (Linebyline Press) 2010, *Poetry That Moves* 2014; "In Her Own Time," *Simple Awakenings* 2010

Joseph Kuhn Carey, "Puffs of Smoke, *Poet's Choice Muses Gallery, Winter 2018*; "Without Electricity," first-place in the Electricity category of the Highland Park Poetry *2018 Poetry Challenge Contest*, and published in the book of the award-winning poems

Susan Spaeth Cherry, "For My Unborn Grandchild," *Sackcloth and Silk: New and Selected Poems* 2017; "Sudden Death," *Trees in This Neighborhood Remember Me* 2017

Kathy Lohrum Cotton, "Breaking the Fast," *Encore Prize Poems* 2016

Charlotte Digregorio, "Winter Dim," winner of the "Wintry Mix" Poetry Contest sponsored by Rockford Writers' Guild, Rockford, IL, March 2017. "My Routine," *After Hours Journal*, Winter 2017

Mary Ann Eiler, "From the poetess to the reader" and "The vagaries of love" were translated from her poems in French, from the chapbook *The sanctity of words, the impiety of speech*

Maureen Tolman Flannery, "Death by Poetry," *Buffalo Bones, California Quarterly, Margin, Poetryfish, Pudding House*, and *Umbrella*

Mike Freveletti, "Humerus," *Snapdragon Journal* 2017

Marilyn Huntman Giese, "gates without a fence," *DuPage Valley Review* 2017

Frank Hubeny, "Advent Darkness," *Ancient Paths Literary Magazine* 2017

Melissa Huff, "A Warning to Pain," *Glass: Facets of Poetry*, Issue 5 – Summer 2017; "Movements at Dusk," *River Poets Journal* 2017: Vol 11 Issue 1

Lennart Lundh, "Sisyphus Discusses…", *National Poetry Month* 2013; "IED QED," *So Careless of Themselves*

Cassandra McGovern, "No Good Deed and All That Jazz," *Fresh Pipes* of the Blue Hill Writer's Group, 2012

Wilda Morris, "Nightmare: A Snake Poem," *Rockford Review*, Winter-Spring 2017; "Grandmother's Bread" online *Alimentum*, November 2015

Donna O'Shaughnessy, "Drawing of My Kindergarten Boyfriend…," *The Galway Review, 2017*; "Handiwork" *Dodging the Rain* 2018

Donna Pucciani, "Pentecost," *Common Ground Review*, then *Edges* by Donna Pucciani, Purple Flag Press, 2016); "After the Solstice," *Flint Hills Review* 2015, *Edges 2016*

Jenene Ravesloot, "Ballena Vallarta," *Art Gets In Your Eyes* 2017; "Found" in *Central Coast Poetry Shows* 2018

Barbara Robinette, "Affirmation," *The Penwood Review* 2016

Tom Roby IV, "Photo Op, Early Evening," *The Muses Gallery* 2017; "Find Me," *Shape Shifter* 2008

Nancy Ann Schaefer, "Headscarves & Tiaras," *Living at hope's edge* 2018

Irfanulla Shariff, "Stormy Night," ISPS website and *Poems of the World* summer issue 2017; "Pomegranate," *PoemHunter* website, January 4, 2018

Beth Staas, "Stuck," *The Lyric* Vol 94 no. 2, Spring 2014

Jennifer Thiermann, "dinner table" and "a thank-you letter," *The Sacred in Contemporary Haiku* 2014; "cattle train," *Every Chicken, Cow, Fish and Frog: Animal Rights Haiku* 2016; "moonlit granite," *Modern Haiku* Vol. 48:3 Autumn 2017; "moonrise," *Frogpond* Vol 40:3 2017; "overnight snow," *Modern Haiku* Summer Vol 46:3 2015

Judith Tullis, "Kabul Dead End," *Poetry That Moves*, August 2015

Curt Vevang, "At the Dollar Store," *the nature of things* 2017; "Half Way Up the Mountain," *a scant bagatelle* 2016

19810119R00085

Made in the USA
Lexington, KY
30 November 2018